EARTH & SPACE SCIENCES

Understanding Volcanoes and Earthquakes

by
Helen Sillett

Don Johnston Incorporated
Volo, Illinois

Edited by:

John Bergez
Start-to-Finish Core Content Series Editor, Pacifica, California

Alan Venable, MA
Start-to-Finish Core Content Developmental Editor, San Francisco, California

Gail Portnuff Venable, MS, CCC-SLP
Speech/Language Pathologist, San Francisco, California

Dorothy Tyack, MA
Learning Disabilities Specialist, San Francisco, California

Jerry Stemach, MS, CCC-SLP
Speech/Language Pathologist, Director of Content Development, Sonoma County, California

Graphics and Illustrations:

Photographs and illustrations are all created professionally and modified to provide the best possible support for the intended reader.
Front Cover, Pages 5, 19, 61, Back Cover: J.D Griggs, U.S. Department of Interior, U.S. Geological Survey
Page 4: G.E. Ulrich, U.S. Department of Interior, U.S. Geological Survey
Page 24: Photo courtesy of 18th Air Base Photo Laboratory, Wheeler Field, Territory of Hawai, U.S. Department of Interior, U.S. Geological Survey
Page 28: Th. Lesales/mount-pelee.com
Pages 29, 56, Back Cover: R.M. Krimmel, U.S. Department of Interior, U.S. Geological Survey
Pages 30: Lipman, P.W., and Mullineaux, D.R., Figure 293-D, U.S. Geological Survey Professional Paper 1250, U.S. Department of Interior, U.S. Geological Survey
Page 34: D. Cavit, U.S. Department of Interior, U.S. Geological Survey
Page 35, Back Cover: W.C. Mendenhall, U.S. Department of Interior, U.S. Geological Survey
Page 36, 50: © CORBIS
Page 38: G.K. Gilbert, U.S. Department of Interior, U.S. Geological Survey
Page 47: W.R. Hansen, U.S. Department of Interior, U.S. Geological Survey
Page 52: © YURIKO NAKAO/Reuters/Corbis
Page 60: R.B. Moore, U.S. Department of Interior, U.S. Geological Survey
Page 62: R. Lapointe, U.S. Air Force
Page 64: C.J. Langer, U.S. Geological Survey
Pages 65, 66, 67: © Bettmann/CORBIS
All other photos © Don Johnston Incorporated and its licensors.

Narration:

Professional actors and actresses read the text to build excitement and to model research-based elements of fluency: intonation, stress, prosody, phrase groupings and rate. The rate has been set to maximize comprehension for the reader.

Published by:

Don Johnston Incorporated
26799 West Commerce Drive
Volo, IL 60073

800.999.4660 USA Canada
800.889.5242 Technical Support
www.donjohnston.com

International Standard Book Number
ISBN 1-4105-0417-4

Table of Contents

Introduction: Shake, Rattle, and Boom 4

Chapter One
Earth Is Always Changing 7

Chapter Two
What Causes Volcanoes? 16

Chapter Three
A Monster Volcano 26

Chapter Four
What Causes Earthquakes? 33

Chapter Five
Monster Earthquakes 40

Chapter Six
**Killer Waves and Other Long Distance
Damage.** 49

Chapter Seven
Fighting Volcanoes and Earthquakes 59

Glossary 69

Introduction: Shake, Rattle, and Boom

How do you know when you're too close to a volcano that is erupting?

A volcano lights up the sky.

Look out! Red-hot rivers of melted rock are coming at you down the mountain. Thick smoke pours out as burning ashes and giant rocks fly down at you from the sky. But that's not all. In a volcanic eruption, the ground shakes beneath your feet. Rocks boom and thunder as they explode. Black clouds of gas shoot out the volcano's mouth. If you're standing in the way of one of those clouds, it will choke you to death and burn your body to a crisp in an instant.

This spray of hot melted rock was 1000 feet high.

Earthquakes are another great danger on our planet. What is it like to go through a large quake? Imagine the ground jumping and rolling beneath you like waves rolling and crashing onto the shore, or buildings falling around you, crushing the people inside. In a strong quake, giant cracks may open in the ground as rocks and mud roll down hills, burying people in their path. Along the shore, cliffs may fall into the sea.

Volcanic eruptions and earthquakes are so powerful and frightening that ancient people made up myths and legends to explain them. Long ago in Japan, people believed that earthquakes were caused by a giant catfish that lived underground.

They believed that on most days, a powerful god watched the catfish carefully. But if the god stopped watching the catfish, the fish thrashed around, and this caused an earthquake.

In ancient Greece, people thought that earthquakes and volcanoes were caused by winds that were trapped under the ground. The ancient Romans believed that a god named Vulcan used the heat inside volcanoes to melt metal for making his weapons. The word volcano is related to the name of the god Vulcan, and a person who studies volcanoes has a similar name — vulcanologist or **volcanologist**.

Today we know a lot more about volcanoes and earthquakes than ancient people did, but these movements from deep in the Earth are still dangerous, and they still fill people with terror.

What causes these **natural disasters**? What damage can they do? And what can be done to protect us from them? To understand these amazing forces of nature, we first have to look at how Earth changes over time.

Chapter One

Earth Is Always Changing

Questions this chapter will answer:

- **What did Earth look like millions of years ago?**

- **How is Earth like an egg?**

- **What is plate tectonics?**

The picture on the right shows three of Earth's continents — North America, South America, and Africa. Do you notice anything about the three shapes?

In 1912, a scientist named Alfred Wegener studied these shapes. Wegener noticed that they seemed to fit together like the pieces of a jigsaw puzzle, and he had an idea about why they fit together so well.

Wegener's work led to a whole new understanding of Earth and a new understanding of volcanoes and earthquakes.

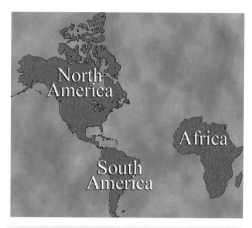

This picture shows the continents of Africa, North America, and South America.

What do you notice about the shapes of the continents if you imagine them closer together?

One Giant Continent

So why do North America, South America, and Africa look like connecting pieces of a jigsaw puzzle? Wegener believed that it was because they were once connected and formed one giant continent. In fact, he believed that *all* the land on Earth had been one giant continent, and he called this giant continent **Pangea**.

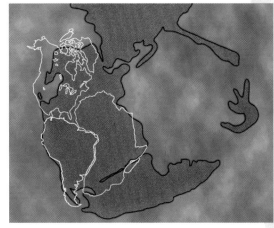

Pangea

The word Pangea comes from two Greek root words: *pan*, meaning "all," and *gea*, meaning "land." Two other words that come from *gea* are **geology** and **geologist**. Geology is the study of how Earth changes over time, and a geologist is a scientist who studies these changes.

Wegener's **theory** was that Pangea broke into pieces millions of years ago, and the pieces drifted apart. A theory is an explanation of something we observe in the natural world. Wegener called his theory **continental drift**.

The shape of the continents was the first big clue that led Wegener to the theory that all the continents had once been connected. Another clue came from ancient **fossils** that were found in South America and Africa.

A fossil is a part of an animal or plant that has hardened into rock, or left its shape in a rock, over many, many years. Fossils are often found in layers of rock. The clue was that fossils of the same ancient plant were found on two different continents, near the eastern coast of South America and near the western coast of Africa.

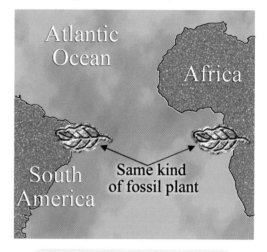

A clue from ancient fossils

Wegener asked himself why the same kind of fossil would be found on opposite sides of the Atlantic Ocean. His answer was that the plant had spread over the land of both continents when they were still connected, before they drifted apart.

Wegener used these and other clues in trying to prove his theory of Pangea and continental drift. For the rest of his life, he tried to get other geologists to accept these ideas, but when he died in 1930, most scientists still did not agree with him.

Today, geologists believe that Wegener was right. More than 200 million years ago, there was only one big continent — a **supercontinent**. But what made that supercontinent break up and move apart into smaller pieces?

An Earth-Sized Egg

To understand how parts of a continent can move, you first need to know what Earth is like on the inside and on the outside.

According to geologists, this is what you would see if you cut a section out of Earth.

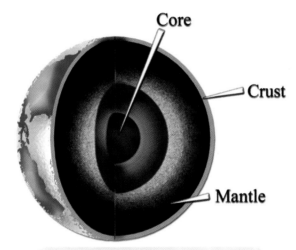

Core

Crust

Mantle

Earth's core, mantle, and crust

Earth has three main parts. They look a bit like the parts of a hard-boiled egg — shell on the outside, egg white under the shell, and egg yolk in the middle.

The outside part of Earth is its crust, like the shell on the egg. You'd need to dig 20 to 50 miles into the ground to reach the bottom of the crust.

The next part of Earth is called the mantle, which lies below the crust. The mantle is much thicker than the crust.

You'd have to dig nearly 2000 miles to get through the mantle. But you wouldn't want to do that, because the mantle is made of partly molten (melted) rock and metal. How hot is molten rock? One system of measuring temperature is called Celsius degrees. Look at these Celsius numbers to get a feel for how hot the mantle is:

- A warm summer day is about 25 degrees Celsius.

- Water boils at 100 degrees Celsius.

- Wood burns at 450 degrees Celsius.

- Earth's molten mantle is about 1200 degrees Celsius.

The third main part of Earth is the core. It's the inside center of Earth, like the yolk at the center of the egg. There are two parts to the core: an outer part that's liquid and an inner part that's solid metal. The liquid outer core is 4000 to 6000 degrees Celsius. The solid inner core is even hotter — about 7000 degrees Celsius.

Sliding Crust

Let's take a closer look at Earth's outer layer — the crust. There are giant cracks in the crust. The cracks form the edges or boundaries of about twelve huge separate pieces of crust. These pieces of crust are called tectonic plates.

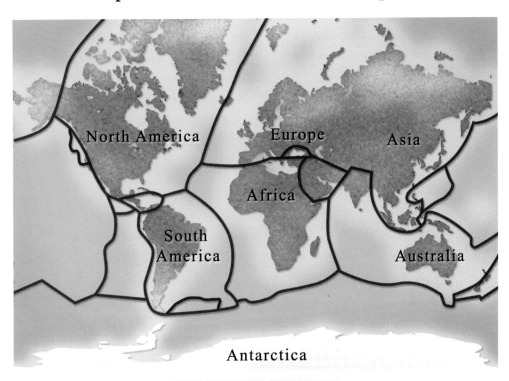

Earth's tectonic plates

Geologists now know that these plates don't stay in one place. They are always moving around, very slowly, about as fast as your fingernails grow. They are constantly sliding past each other, moving away, or crashing together.

13

Scientists have a name for this movement. They call it **plate tectonics**.

Why does plate tectonics happen? Why are the plates always moving? Geologists don't know for sure. They think it's because of the hot, molten mantle lying underneath Earth's crust. The partly melted hot rock of the mantle is slowly moving, too. The mantle is like a pot of chunky soup that is boiling on the stove. Now imagine some crackers floating on the surface of the soup. These are like Earth's plates. As the soup gently bubbles, the crackers move around on the surface of the soup.

Geologists now know that plate tectonics led to the break-up of Pangea. Over millions of years, the movement of the plates broke up the supercontinent. The pieces are the continents we have today.

Plate tectonics can also create mountains and valleys by raising or lowering the surface of the crust. Many of Earth's **mountain ranges** were formed by plate tectonics. A mountain range is a line or group of mountains that are next to each other. When two plates collide (hit each other), they can bend and fold and buckle along their boundaries (edges). Even though the plates are moving slowly, they sometimes collide like two cars hitting each other head-on. The highest mountain range in the world, the Himalayas, rose up because of tectonic plates slowly colliding along their boundaries. When plates collide, we call it **plate collision**.

The continents are still moving today because of plate tectonics. Geologists have an idea of how the continents may look in 250 million years. They think that five of Earth's continents will join back together into a giant continent, like a new Pangea.

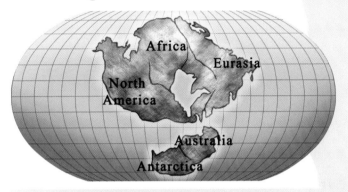

What Earth might look like in 250 million years

Chapter Summary

In this chapter, you read about Alfred Wegener and his idea that, millions of years ago, one giant continent broke up into the continents we know today. You learned about Earth's three layers — hard outer crust, molten mantle, and core. The crust is made up of twelve giant plates that are slowly moving around. Wegener called this movement continental drift. Today, we call it plate tectonics.

You may be wondering, "What do moving plates have to do with volcanic eruptions and earthquakes?" The answer is that plate tectonics causes most of them. In the next chapter, you'll learn how plate tectonics causes volcanoes to form.

Chapter Two

What Causes Volcanoes?

Questions this chapter will answer:

- What do all volcanoes have in common?

- How do moving plates cause volcanoes to erupt?

- Where do hot spot volcanoes form?

If a volcano still erupts from time to time, it is called an active volcano.

A map of Earth's active volcanoes in 2005

This map has red marks showing the places where active volcanoes are found.

Before you continue to read, look carefully at where these volcanoes are. Do you notice any patterns?

You might notice that many of the volcanoes are found along the edges of Earth's major plates. And do you notice how many volcanoes there are around the edges of the Pacific Ocean? That line of volcanoes has a special name: the Ring of Fire.

In this chapter, you'll read about why volcanoes form and erupt where they do.

Molten Rock

Volcanoes come in many different shapes and sizes, but they all have one thing in common. All volcanoes are formed by hot molten rock called magma. Without magma, there would be no volcanoes. A car needs gas to drive, and a volcano needs magma to erupt.

Magma forms in Earth's mantle, or middle layer. Gas is often mixed in with the magma. After the gas and magma form, they rise up through the crust. As molten magma pours up through the crust to the surface, it becomes a volcano.

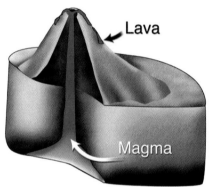

Inside a volcano

When the magma gets near the surface of Earth, it collects in chambers (pockets) inside the crust. As more and more magma and gas pour into a chamber, the pressure in the chamber grows because the magma and gas are pressing against the walls of the chamber, trying to get out.

It's a bit like a can of soda. What happens when you shake a can of soda before you open it? The pressure of gas in the soda builds up inside the can. The soda gas is trying to push out of the can, so when you open the can, the soda will spray everywhere. As magma builds up in the chamber inside Earth's crust, the magma and gas get ready to break out and spray.

When the pressure gets too high, the chamber can no longer hold back the magma and gas. They begin to squeeze up through the crust, forcing their way out through weak spots in the crust until they reach the surface. When the magma comes out on the surface, volcanologists give it a different name: lava. As the lava builds up on the surface, the volcano begins to grow.

Lava spraying out of a volcano in Hawaii

Plates Crashing Together or Pulling Apart

In the last chapter, you read about the tectonic plates that make up the surface of Earth. It is the movement of these plates that creates most of the volcanoes on Earth. Some of these volcanoes are formed when the plates crash into each other along their boundaries, and others are formed when the plates pull apart from each other.

Let's look first at how volcanoes are formed when Earth's plates come together. This picture shows you what can happen underneath the surface when two plates collide.

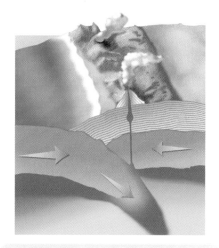

When plates collide, one plate may slide under the other.

Sometimes when the plates collide, one of the plates slides under the other. The plate that is forced underneath gets pushed down into Earth's hot mantle. There, the edge of the plate begins to melt and turn into magma. Earlier in this chapter, you read about what happens next. The magma rises up through the mantle and then up through the crust until it erupts on the surface, forming a volcano.

Let's look now at the volcanoes that are formed when two plates pull apart from each other. As two plates move away from each other, a long crack opens in Earth's crust. A crack like this runs under the Atlantic Ocean and through the middle of Iceland.

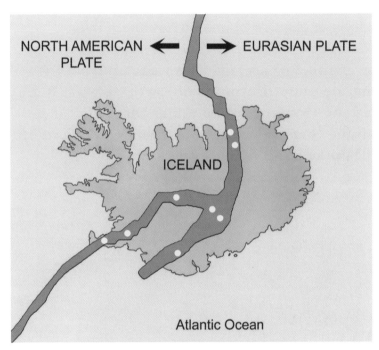

A long crack in Earth's crust.
The yellow dots are volcanoes.

The crack is there because two plates are moving away from each other at a rate of about one inch each year.

As the plates move apart, magma may rise up through the crack. When it does, a new volcano is formed.

Hot Spot Volcanoes

Volcanologists say that most volcanoes form along the edges of plates, as you have just read. That's why we have the Ring of Fire. But there is another type of volcano, the hot spot volcano.

Hot spot volcanoes don't form along the edges of Earth's plates. They form over something called a plume. A plume is a column or channel of magma that rises up from the mantle underneath one of Earth's plates. It may rise up from any place under the plate. If a plume comes up under the ocean, an island of lava may build up over the plume.

As lava flows out through a plate, it hardens. After many eruptions and many layers of lava, a volcanic mountain begins to form. The lava builds and builds under the water until an island peeks out above the ocean.

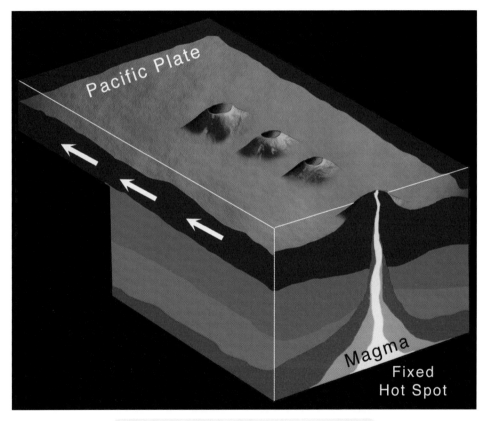

How hot spot volcanoes are formed

All the islands of Hawaii were formed by a single hot spot. How did this happen? The hot spot always stays in the same place in the mantle, but the plate (the crust) above the hot spot is slowly moving.

23

After the hot spot formed one volcanic island, the plate slowly drifted to the northwest, and, because the volcanic island was *on* the plate, the island slowly drifted away from the hot spot. But then a new part of the plate was sitting above the hot spot, so as the hot spot continued to erupt, a whole new volcanic island was formed.

Today, the Hawaiian island called the Big Island is over the hot spot. There are two active volcanoes on the Big Island.

The largest active volcano is Mauna Loa in Hawaii. It rises up 5.5 miles from the ocean floor.

You may have read about the Galapagos Islands. The Galapagos Islands were formed by hot spot volcanoes, too.

Chapter Summary

In this chapter, you read about how volcanoes are formed. In all volcanoes, hot magma comes up and turns into lava. Most of Earth's volcanoes are formed around the edges of the plates in its crust, where the tectonic plates are hitting each other or moving apart. Hot spot volcanoes come from plumes in the mantle and can happen away from the edges of plates.

In the next chapter, you'll read about a single moment one hundred years ago when a volcano killed 29,000 people.

Chapter Three

A Monster Volcano

Questions this chapter will answer:

- **What clues did Mount Pelée give when it was about to erupt?**

- **How did people nearby react to the clues?**

"The mountain was blown to pieces.... The side of the volcano was ripped out, and ... a solid wall of flame ... flew straight toward us. It sounded like a thousand cannons. The wave of fire was on us and over us like a lightning flash."

These are the words of Charles Thompson. In 1902, Thompson saw a volcano erupt. It was a hundred years ago, but it still stands out as one of the worst eruptions of modern times.

The volcano that erupted on that day is called Mount Pelée. Mount Pelée is an old volcanic mountain on the island of Martinique in the Caribbean Sea. There are a lot of volcanoes in this part of the Caribbean because two of Earth's plates are colliding there, between North and South America.

Mount Pelée erupted about one hundred years ago.

Thompson was a member of the crew of a steamship that was anchored just off the island when the volcano erupted. He was lucky to survive. More than 29,000 people were killed. Let's see what happened on that terrible day.

27

Clues that the Volcano Was Going to Erupt

Volcanologists say the volcano gave many clues that it was going to erupt.

The first clue began a few years before the eruption. Before an eruption, toxic (poisonous) gas sometimes escapes from the magma inside a volcano. Mount Pelée had started giving off toxic gas. The gas came out of cracks near the top of the mountain. It was a sign that magma was moving up inside.

Mount Pelée today

How did people know that the volcano was giving off gas? The gas had something called sulfur in it, and sulfur smells like rotten eggs. Wind carried the smell to the people in a nearby village.

The people also had another way of knowing that the volcano was giving off toxic gas. Birds that were flying over the volcano suddenly died and fell from the sky. They were killed by breathing the gas.

The volcano gave a second clue that it was about to erupt. The mountain started to grow in size. People didn't know it at the time, but this was also a sign that magma was moving up inside the volcano. The fresh magma made the volcano swell up.

There were other clues, too. In the month before the eruption, there were many small earthquakes around Mount Pelée. When magma moves up inside a volcano, the magma can crack and break rocks in the Earth's crust. This can make the ground shake all around the volcano.

Smoke and ash pouring out of a volcano (Mount St. Helens in the state of Washington, 1980)

Then, closer to the time of the eruption, smoke poured out of the volcano, and people saw flashes of fire near the top. Ash rained down on the land around the volcano. Many of the animals that lived on the volcano began to flee. Millions of ants, snakes, and centipedes came crawling down the mountain.

29

The City That Didn't Believe

About three miles from the volcano was the city of St. Pierre, home to 29,000 people. Of course, the people knew that the volcano was giving off gas and ash, because their eyes and throats were sore from the sulfur. They walked around with wet cloths over their faces to keep out the gas and ash. Everything was coated in white ash, as if a snowstorm had hit the city.

But even with all the clues, most people in St. Pierre didn't believe that Mount Pelée was about to erupt. It hadn't erupted for more than 50 years, and the last eruption hadn't been serious, just a shower of ash. So people didn't pay much attention to what was happening this time.

Then, on May 8th, 1902, at 8 o'clock in the morning, the volcano cut loose with four giant explosions. Smoke and ash poured out of the mountain up into the sky.

Then a brown gas blasted out of the mountain. This cloud was super-hot — probably about 900 degrees Celsius! It also carried drops of hot magma and small chunks of rock.

Clouds of ash after a pyroclastic flow (Mount St. Helens, 1980)

The toxic, super-hot brown cloud raced down the mountain at 200 miles an hour like a hurricane of fire.

Scientists call this kind of cloud a **pyroclastic flow**. It doesn't happen in every volcanic eruption. This is a good thing, because pyroclastic flows are killers.

The blast raced down the mountainside and across the island, heading straight for St. Pierre. The super-hot flow set fields and trees on fire. In only a few seconds, the burning winds reached the city.

The blast set fire to St. Pierre, burning it to the ground. Almost all the people in the city were killed in an instant.

The city of St. Pierre was destroyed by the volcano.

Only one man survived — a man named Auguste. When the blast hit the town, Auguste was in jail. His cell had very thick stone walls and one small window that faced away from Mount Pelée. The cell helped to protect him from the force of the blast, but he was badly burned. He had to wait for four days without food or water before he was rescued.

Later on, Auguste was let out of jail and he joined a circus in the United States. In the circus, he sat in a cell as part of an act about the volcano.

Chapter Summary

In this chapter, you read about Mount Pelée, a volcano that erupted about one hundred years ago, killing 29,000 people. There were many clues that an eruption was near, but the people didn't pay attention to the clues. When the volcano erupted, a pyroclastic flow spread fire across the island, and only one man survived.

So far you've learned about tectonic plates, volcanic eruptions, magma, and lava. The next chapter explains why earthquakes happen.

Chapter Four

What Causes Earthquakes?

Questions this chapter will answer:

- **What kind of movement causes earthquakes?**

- **What is an earthquake zone?**

Take a look at this picture of a field on a farm in a part of California called the Imperial Valley. The picture was taken in 1979. Do you notice anything strange about it?

What threw the furrows in this field out of line?

Before farmers plant seeds, they plow the field. The plow cuts the soil into long straight rows called furrows. Just before this picture was taken, the furrows in this field were straight. But then something threw the furrows out of line. It looks as if half of the field slid one way and the other half of the field slid the other way.

Think about what you know about the plates on Earth's surface. Before you continue reading, take a guess about how the furrows in this field moved out of line.

Moving Plates and Earthquakes

Just like volcanoes, most earthquakes happen near the edges of Earth's tectonic plates. At the edges, the plates rub against each other or slide under each other. These movements of the plates cause earthquakes.

The tectonic plates are always moving, causing thousands of tiny earthquakes every day around the world. Most of these quakes are too small for anyone to feel, but sometimes the plates move more suddenly or jump a longer distance. When this happens, people notice the ground shaking and feel the jolt of an earthquake — maybe even a big one.

This picture was taken in San Francisco in 1906 after a big quake shook the city.

Why do tectonic plates sometimes move suddenly or jump? It happens because the edges of the plates aren't smooth and straight; they're rocky, rough, and bumpy. As the plates slide past each other or under each other, the plates may get stuck on a rough spot. The rest of the giant plates keep sliding along, but the plates can't move in the places where they are stuck.

35

As time goes by, the pressure builds and builds in the place where the plates are stuck. The plates are straining to break free. The part of each plate that is stuck is straining to catch up with the rest of its plate. Finally, a stuck part breaks and the plates suddenly move.

If you've ever been in a tug of war with a friend, you know what this is like.

A tug of war

An Earthquake Zone

Let's take a look at an example of a place where a lot of earthquakes happen because of Earth's moving plates. This amazing picture was taken from the air above an **earthquake zone** in California. The camera was looking down at a **fault** (a crack or line) in the crust of the Earth.

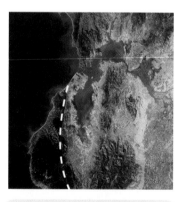

The dotted line in this picture follows a part of the San Andreas fault.

An earthquake zone is an area where scientists expect earthquakes to happen. Most earthquake zones are places where the scientists have been able to find a number of faults. The crack shown in this picture is a part of the San Andreas Fault. The San Andreas Fault was created by the movement of Earth's plates.

California is loaded with earthquake zones because it lies along the west coast of the United States, at the boundaries of two main tectonic plates. Part of California sits on the North American Plate, and the rest of California sits on the Pacific Plate. The North American Plate and the Pacific Plate are sliding along next to each other. They are moving in opposite directions, like two lines of cars moving on opposite sides of a highway.

These cars are moving in opposite directions like two plates sliding past each other.

The North American Plate and the Pacific Plate are moving past each other at an average rate of about 2 inches per year. Imagine that you stand on one plate and your friend stands right across from you on the other plate. If you both stood there for 15 to 20 million years, you and your friend would end up 350 miles apart.

The edge of a tectonic plate is not the same thing as a fault line, but the movement of the plates has caused many faults and cracks in Earth's crust near the edges of the plates. Have you ever cut a pie crust after it's baked? You may have noticed how hard it is to cut a straight line through the crust. Bits of crust crack and break off as you cut. The Earth's crust near the edges of two plates is a bit like the pie after you've cut it.

The movement of tectonic plates can make the ground shift suddenly along a fault. In 1906, a terrible earthquake rocked the San Andreas Fault near the city of San Francisco. This picture was taken after the earthquake. Before the earthquake, the fence in the picture was straight.

Before the 1906 earthquake, this was one long straight fence.

In the earthquake, the ground shifted, causing the two halves of the fence to slide eight feet apart. In another spot, the ground shifted more than 20 feet.

Chapter Summary

In this chapter you read about what causes earthquakes. Most of them happen at the edges of Earth's tectonic plates. These are the places where the plates are rubbing together or sliding under each other. Most earthquakes are too small for people to feel, but when plates make bigger, more sudden movements, people feel the quake.

Faults can be found in earthquake zones, which form along the edges of plates. Earthquakes happen along the faults. The most famous fault in California is called the San Andreas Fault.

Chapter Five

Monster Earthquakes

Questions this chapter will answer:

- **How can we tell how strong an earthquake is?**

- **What was the strongest earthquake that scientists have measured?**

- **What was the second strongest earthquake?**

"Oh boy, oh boy! Man, that's an earthquake! Hey, that's an earthquake for sure! Boy, oh boy … I'm going through it right now! Man! Everything's moving … Who-eee! Scared the hell out of me, man! Oh boy, I wish this house would quit shaking! … I've never lived through anything like this before in my life! … Oooeeee … the whole place is shaking … it's still shaking, I'm telling you! I wonder if I should get outside? Oh boy! Man, I'm telling you that's the worst thing I ever lived through!"

The man who spoke these words lived through the second strongest earthquake in the past 100 years. It happened in 1964, in the state of Alaska. When the quake hit, he was speaking into a tape recorder.

In this chapter, you'll read how earthquakes are measured and what two big quakes were like.

How Strong Was That Earthquake?

Scientists have been studying earthquakes for almost 2000 years. In the year 132, a scientist in China invented the first tool for measuring earthquakes. It was a large metal pot with several metal dragon heads around the outside.

A Chinese invention to measure earthquakes

Each dragon head had a ball in its teeth. When an earthquake happened, one or more of the dragons might drop the ball from its mouth. With this tool, the scientist hoped to be able to tell when an earthquake was happening even if it was too small for him to feel. He also used the pot to figure out which direction the quake came from.

The measurement of earthquakes is much better today. Now earthquakes are measured and recorded on a machine called a **seismograph**. *Seismo* comes from the Greek word for "shock," and *graph* comes from the Greek word for "write." *Seismo* is also part of the word for a scientist who studies earthquakes — a **seismologist**.

Many seismographs have needles that move back and forth when the ground moves or shakes. The more the ground shakes, the farther the needle moves. One end of the needle is a pen that writes on a moving sheet of paper to make a record of each shake. Seismologists study these records to see how strong the shakes were during a quake.

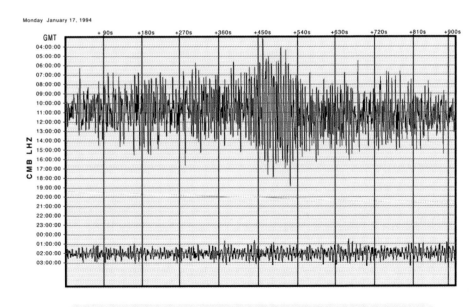

The record of an earthquake on seismograph paper

In the 1930s, a seismologist named Charles Richter suggested a system of numbers for measuring the strength of an earthquake. The strength of an earthquake is called its magnitude. Richter's system helps us to organize the information we get from seismographs. He called his system the Richter Scale. Before seismographs and the Richter Scale, people had no good way to compare the magnitudes of different earthquakes. They had tried to do it by looking at how much damage the earthquakes had done. But this wasn't a good way of measuring magnitude, because a weak earthquake in a city might do more damage than a powerful earthquake in the country.

The Richter Scale has numbers that go from 1 to 10. A small earthquake might score a magnitude of 1 on the Richter Scale. A huge earthquake could score a 7, an 8, or higher.

The numbers on the Richter Scale are a bit tricky to understand. For example, a magnitude score of 2 is not just slightly stronger than a score of 1. In fact, a 2 is *ten times* stronger than a 1 on the Richter Scale. A 3 is ten times stronger than a 2, and *one hundred* times stronger than a 1. As another example, a quake that got a score of 5 on the Richter Scale would be 1000 times stronger than a quake that scored a 2.

The Strongest Quake on the Scale

The strongest quake ever recorded on the Richter Scale happened in 1960 in the country of Chile, in South America. The magnitude of this quake was measured at 9.5. It is possible that there have been stronger earthquakes before this one, but the Richter Scale wasn't around to measure them.

Chile is one of the world's most dangerous volcano and earthquake zones because it's a place where one of Earth's giant plates is sliding under another plate.

The earthquake in Chile was deadly. The **death toll** (number of humans killed) was about 2500 people. Many people in the earthquake zone felt lucky that the death toll wasn't even higher.

Why weren't more people killed? Right before the earthquake hit, there were a few smaller quakes called foreshocks.

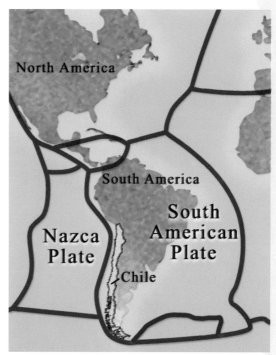

Many earthquakes happen in Chile because two of Earth's giant plates meet there.

45

They are called foreshocks because they come *before* a big shock. Luckily, people felt the foreshocks and ran outside, so they were not caught inside buildings when the big quake hit.

The shaking went on for several minutes. Buildings collapsed. Roads broke into pieces. Cliffs fell into the ocean. Mudslides raced down hills and mountain slopes. The earthquake ripped open the Earth, leaving a crack in the ground that was 500 miles long.

The Second-Strongest Shake

What about the second strongest earthquake on the Richter Scale? In 1964, a quake in Alaska reached a magnitude of 9.2. At the beginning of this chapter, you read the words of a man who survived this monster.

Like Chile, Alaska is in one of the most active earthquake and volcano zones in the world. Alaska is another place where two tectonic plates are colliding and one of the plates is slowly being pushed under the other one.

The Alaska quake began with some gentle shaking. Then the ground moved violently. One person said that the ground looked like the ocean with waves that were three feet high. The shaking went on for almost five minutes, and people said those five minutes felt like forever.

In the Alaska earthquake, many houses, schools and other buildings collapsed, and landslides pushed many homes downhill. A lot of this damage happened at the epicenter of the quake. The epicenter of an earthquake is the ground above the place in the crust where an earthquake starts.

This home was destroyed in the Alaska earthquake of 1964.

The movement of the Earth's plates pushed giant slabs of land up into the air. Seismologists call this uplift. In some places, pieces of land were lifted more than 50 feet into the air.

After the giant earthquake ended, there were more than 50 aftershocks — smaller earthquakes that come *after* a bigger one on the same fault. Eleven of these aftershocks came on the same day as the giant quake, and the rest happened over the next year.

Chapter Summary

In this chapter, you read about how seismologists measure earthquakes using seismographs and the Richter Scale.

You also read about the two strongest earthquakes that have happened since the Richter Scale was invented. The strongest quake took place in Chile in 1960. People there were lucky that the foreshocks gave them a bit of warning. In 1964, there was another strong quake in Alaska. That quake created some very high uplifts and was followed by many aftershocks.

In the next chapter, you'll read about one of the biggest dangers of earthquakes and volcanoes — ocean waves.

Chapter Six

Killer Waves and Other Long Distance Damage

Questions this chapter will answer:

- How can an earthquake kill people thousands of miles away?

- How do earthquakes and volcanoes create killer waves?

- How can a volcano kill people on the other side of the world?

You know that a volcano can kill people with gas and smoke. You know that people can die in earthquakes when buildings and roads collapse. But did you know that volcanoes and earthquakes can kill people who are thousands of miles away from the eruption or the shaking?

Damage from a killer wave that struck the island of Hilo, Hawaii in 1960

The other side of the world may seem far away, but all the living things on Earth are connected to each other. Something that happens in your country can change the lives of people across the planet.

Volcanoes and earthquakes sometimes cause giant killer waves. Let's study one of these killer waves. We'll also look at some of the problems that were caused by huge volcanic eruptions.

Giant Waves

In December 2004, the biggest earthquake in 40 years shook the country of Indonesia. The earthquake was big, but the worst damage happened after the earthquake was over. Hours after the shaking stopped, hundreds of thousands more people were killed. Some of them were 3000 miles away from where the earthquake hit. These people were killed by a group of giant waves, called a **tsunami**.

The center of the earthquake was under the Indian Ocean, about 150 miles off the coast of Indonesia. Indonesia is a group of islands that are south of China. Right after the quake, waves started racing away from where the quake had happened. The waves were moving across the ocean at 500 miles an hour, as fast as a jet plane. In less than an hour, the waves had grown into giant walls of water that slammed into the coast of Indonesia. Soon, the giant waves hit the countries of India, Sri Lanka, and Thailand. Six to seven hours after the earthquake, the waves traveled 3000 miles across the Indian Ocean and hit the coast of Africa.

In 2004, an underwater earthquake sent waves rolling out across the Indian Ocean.

When the waves hit land, some were as tall as 30-50 feet high, higher than a four-story building.

The waves tossed people around as if they were tiny dolls. Waves rolled across towns and poured into houses and hotels, trapping people inside and drowning them. People were also killed when they were hit by heavy objects in the water, like cars, trees, and metal beams. In some places, the water swept away entire towns and most of the people who lived in them.

Damage from the tsunami in Asia in 2004

The 2004 tsunami killed more people than any other tsunami in history. In Indonesia, the country that was closest to where the tsunami started, at least 108,000 people were killed. Imagine a huge outdoor stadium packed with people watching the Olympics, and you'll have some idea of how many were killed when the earthquake and tsunami hit Indonesia.

All around the Indian Ocean, more than 280,000 people were killed by the earthquake and tsunami. More than a million people lost their homes because of the tsunami.

Tsunamis from Earthquakes and Volcanoes

How do earthquakes cause these giant killer waves? If you've ever soaked yourself in a bathtub, you know that water in a tub will slosh around if you move suddenly. An earthquake can cause the ocean to slosh around in a similar way.

Sometimes during an earthquake, the movement of the Earth's plates can lift up a giant slab of the seafloor. The seafloor is the land at the bottom of the ocean. When this uplift happens, the ocean water above the seafloor is also pushed upward.

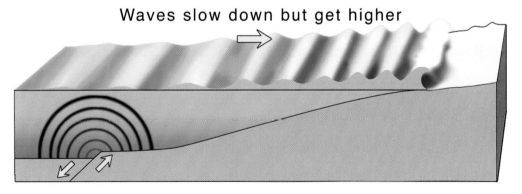

Waves slow down but get higher

This picture shows how a tsunami changes as it gets closer to shore.

This causes big waves to form and start moving quickly across the ocean. Those waves are tsunamis.

In the middle of the ocean, the waves aren't very high. That's because the ocean is very deep and the waves have room to spread out. If you were on a ship in the middle of the ocean and a tsunami passed by, you probably wouldn't even notice it.

But as the waves get closer to land, the ocean gets more shallow, and since the waves can't spread out in the deep ocean any more, they get closer together and begin to slow down. They also begin to lift up above the surface of the water. When the tsunami finally hits land, the waves can be fifty feet high or more.

Earthquakes aren't the only events that can cause tsunamis. A large volcanic eruption in or near the ocean can move the seafloor and start a tsunami. A giant landslide that slips into the ocean can also start a tsunami. Sometimes these giant landslides are set off by earthquakes or volcanoes.

A Blast That Was Felt Around the World

In 1815, a volcano called Tambora erupted violently. Right away, the blast killed 10,000 people who lived near the volcano. But the effects of the volcano went much farther. The eruption was so big that it caused problems for countries around the world.

Tambora was on an island called Sumbawa. Today, the island is part of Indonesia.

A volcano on the island of Sumbawa caused damage around the world.

55

The volcanic blast sent a huge cloud of smoke and ash more than 20 miles up into the air. The ash in the air around the volcano completely blocked out the sun. For hundreds of miles around the volcano, the sky was as black as night for three days.

In 1815, when Tambora erupted, there were no cameras, but this photo might help you imagine what the eruption looked like. Tambora put out 80 times more lava, smoke, gas, and ash than the eruption of Mount St. Helens that you see in this photo.

The dust and gas rose into the **atmosphere** (the blanket of air around the Earth), where they acted as a kind of shield. The shield blocked out much of the sun's light and warmth. On the islands near the volcano, crops died because they didn't get enough sunlight. This led to **famine** (people starving because they didn't have enough to eat). High in the atmosphere, winds carried the volcanic dust and gas around the globe. In this way, the effects of the volcano were felt all the way around the world.

For the next two to three years, temperatures around the world went down. In the United States, there were snowstorms and frost in the summer months of June, July, and August. Snow also fell in Europe in the summer. The snow was brown, yellow, or a reddish color because of the volcanic dust in the atmosphere.

The strange cold weather destroyed crops all around the world. This led to famine far away from Sumbawa. People became weak from lack of food, and this allowed many diseases to spread.

About 10,000 people were killed in the blast of Tambora, but the same eruption may actually have killed as many as 82,000 more people around the world through famine and disease.

Chapter Summary

In this chapter, you read about some effects of volcanoes and earthquakes.

Earthquakes and volcanoes sometimes cause tsunamis. In 2004, an earthquake near Indonesia sent a deadly tsunami rolling thousands of miles out across the Indian Ocean.

The volcanic eruption of Tambora in 1815 made temperatures around the world go down. And in places far away from the eruption, crops were destroyed by cold weather, leading to famines and disease.

Studying volcanoes and earthquakes like these, gives scientists important information. In the next chapter, you'll read about how scientists are trying to use this information to save lives.

Chapter Seven

Fighting Volcanoes and Earthquakes

Questions this chapter will answer:

- **How are volcanologists trying to save people from volcanoes?**

- **How are scientists trying to save people from earthquakes and tsunamis?**

- **How did cold water save a town in Iceland?**

In 1993, a group of volcanologists climbed a volcano in the country of Colombia, along the Ring of Fire. Before starting out, they checked to make sure that the volcano wasn't showing any signs of erupting. They thought that they were safe. But they were wrong. The mountain was about to blow.

At the top of the volcano, the scientists went about their work. Suddenly, the ground started to shake.

"Run!" yelled one of the scientists, a man named Stan Williams. Everyone ran for their lives.

Stan could run only a few yards before he heard a giant boom and saw his leg crushed by a huge red-hot rock, while the rest of his body was burned by hot gas. Later, he was rescued from the volcano, but it was two years before he could walk again. Six other volcanologists died in the blast, so Stan was lucky to be alive.

Around the world, scientists like Stan Williams are trying to figure out the secrets of volcanoes and earthquakes.

Scientists risk their lives to understand volcanoes. This photo was taken on Mauna Loa Volcano in Hawaii in 1984.

In this chapter, you'll read about how science is saving lives and property in the battle against earthquakes and volcanoes.

The Main Thing Is Knowing When

Scientists are trying many tools to **predict** (guess ahead of time) when a volcano is likely to erupt.

A volcanologist collects a sample of hot lava from an erupting volcano.

They use seismographs to **monitor** (keep checking) the land around the volcano. As you have seen, a seismograph measures and records any movement or shaking in the ground. Scientists know that if the ground starts shaking, an eruption may be on the way.

They use other machines to test the atmosphere around the volcano. If they find toxic gases in the air, they know that the volcano may be getting ready to blow.

In 1991, scientists saved the lives of about 70,000 people in a country called the Philippines, which also lies on the Ring of Fire. A volcano called Pinatubo was giving off toxic gases. The scientists warned the people who lived around the volcano to flee to safety. Soon after this, Pinatubo erupted. It was the biggest eruption in more than 75 years.

When Pinatubo erupted, it sent giant clouds of smoke and ash into the sky.

But scientists don't always know when a volcano will erupt. At the beginning of this chapter, you read about a volcano that erupted without giving any warning signs. The scientists had checked for gas and earth movements before they climbed the volcano that day.

The volcano had seemed safe, but some of the scientists ended up dead.

Sometimes a volcano acts like it is going to erupt, but then it doesn't. This is dangerous, too, because if scientists tell people to flee, and then the volcano doesn't blow, people may not believe the scientists the next time they give a warning.

Saving Lives from Earthquakes and Tsunamis

Earthquakes can destroy cities and kill thousands of people in an instant. But, thanks to modern science, we have information that can make us safer. For example, we know more now about how earthquakes behave and how buildings respond to quakes. Scientists are using this information to save lives by designing buildings that won't collapse. Today, many cities around the world have strict rules or laws that builders must follow to make buildings safer during earthquakes. For example, high-rise buildings are built to sway back and forth during an earthquake, but not collapse. These rules or laws are called **building codes**.

In 1988, an earthquake hit a country named Armenia. Because there weren't strict building codes, about 25,000 people were killed in the quake. Many died inside buildings that collapsed on top of them.

A collapsed church in Armenia
after the earthquake of 1988

Scientists have also set up a system to warn people about tsunamis. When an earthquake or an eruption sets off a tsunami, warnings are sent to all the places that might be hit. These warnings give people time to evacuate (get away from) the shoreline and move to higher ground that the waves won't reach.

Doing Battle Against a Volcano

People are also finding ways to do more than just run away from volcanoes.

In 1973, a volcano erupted on a small island that belonged to Iceland. Not far from the volcano, there was a fishing town with more than 5000 people. Right away, the people were evacuated to safety. But safety was just one part of the problem. This town had the busiest fishing port in Iceland. If the volcano destroyed the port and its harbor, the whole country would lose a lot of money.

The volcano was close to a fishing town. Here you see volcanic ash sweeping over the town.

Many homes were crushed or burned by the burning rocks and ash that flew out of the volcano. Soon, lava began flowing toward the town. The lava was thick, and it was filled with giant chunks of rock. Everybody was worried that this wall of lava would swallow the town and destroy the port.

Ash covers the main street of the town.

65

Scientists decided to try something new to save the town and the port. When lava cools down, it gets thicker and thicker and finally hardens into rock. "What if we could find a way to cool down the lava?" the scientists wondered. "Then maybe we could stop the lava from destroying the town."

The Iceland volcano erupting

The seawater near Iceland is very cold. The scientists decided to try to use this icy water to cool down the lava. They put a ship in the harbor, and the ship pumped water out of the sea. From there, a giant hose was used to spray the water over the lava. As the cold water hit the hot lava, the water turned to steam.

This first step in the plan seemed to work. The lava that was sprayed with water cooled and became thicker. The flow began to move more slowly. After a while, the lava piled up on itself instead of moving forward.

The scientists quickly decided to bring in more pumps and spray more water on the lava. About 75 men worked around the clock to spray the lava with millions of gallons of water. For four months, they kept on spraying.

The battle against the lava was a success. About a third of the town was destroyed by the volcano, but the rest of the town was saved. The port and the harbor were also saved. Scientists hope to use the same solution to fight other volcanoes in the future.

This wall of lava destroyed
many buildings in the town.

67

Chapter Summary

In this chapter, you read about how scientists are using new information to save lives. Volcanologists are trying to figure out ways to tell when a volcano is going to erupt. Cities use building codes so that buildings will be less likely to collapse during an earthquake. Warnings about tsunamis tell people when they need to evacuate to higher, safer ground. In a battle against a volcano in Iceland, scientists used cold sea water to save a town from a flow of lava.

There are still many things that we don't know about volcanoes and earthquakes. We still don't know exactly when they are going to happen. But we're learning more all the time. Scientists hope that the studies they are doing now will help them to make better predictions about these natural disasters in the future and save more lives.

Glossary

Word	Definition	Page
active volcano	a volcano that still erupts from time to time	17
aftershock	an earthquake that happens soon after another earthquake along the same fault	47
atmosphere	the blanket of air around the Earth	56
building codes	rules or laws that builders must follow to make buildings safer during earthquakes	63
continental drift	All the land on Earth is slowly moving. We call this continental drift.	9
core	the center part of the Earth	12
crust	the outside part of the Earth	11
death toll	the number of people who are killed during an earthquake, volcano, or some other terrible event	45
earthquake zone	an area where scientists expect earthquakes to happen	36
epicenter	the ground that is above the place in the crust where an earthquake starts	47

Word	Definition	Page
evacuate	to get away from a dangerous place	64
famine	When people die because they don't have enough food to eat, we call this a famine.	56
fault	a crack or line in the Earth's crust	36
fossil	A fossil is a part of an animal or plant that has hardened into rock, or left its shape in a rock, over many, many years.	9
geologist	a scientist who studies how Earth changes over time	9
geology	the study of how Earth changes over time	9
lava	molten rock that has poured out on to the Earth's surface	19
magma	molten rock that is below the surface of the Earth	18
magnitude	the strength of an earthquake	44
mantle	the part of the Earth that is below the crust	11
monitor	to keep checking something carefully	61

Word	Definition	Page
molten rock	melted rock	18
mountain range	a line or group of mountains that are next to each other	14
natural disaster	a terrible event, like an earthquake or flood, that is caused by nature	6
Pangea	All the land on Earth was once connected together in a giant continent known as Pangea.	9
plate collision	When the pieces of Earth's crust collide, we call this plate collision.	14
plate tectonics	The pieces of Earth's crust are always moving. This movement is called plate tectonics.	14
plume	a channel of magma that rises up from the mantle underneath one of Earth's plates	22
predict	to guess what will happen	61
pyroclastic flow	a cloud of hot gas that blasts out of a volcano and moves very fast	31
Richter Scale	a system of numbers for measuring earthquakes	44

Word	Definition	Page
Ring of Fire	a line of **volcanoes** around the edges of the Pacific Ocean, where some of Earth's plates are colliding with each other	17
seismograph	a machine for measuring and recording earthquakes	43
seismologist	a scientist who studies earthquakes	43
supercontinent	one huge continent	10
tectonic plates	the pieces of Earth's **crust**	13
theory	an idea that explains something that we see in the natural world	9
toxic gas	a gas that hurts or kills people when they breathe it	28
tsunami	a giant wave that can be caused by **volcanoes** and earthquakes	51
uplift	giant slabs of land being pushed up by the movement of the Earth's **tectonic plates**	47
volcanic eruption	When smoke, gas, or molten rock pour out of a **volcano**, we call this a volcanic eruption.	5

Word	Definition	Page
volcano	an opening in Earth's **crust** where smoke, gas, or molten rock can pour out	4
volcanologist	a scientist who studies **volcanoes**	6

About the Author

Helen Sillett was born in England and lived in the Netherlands and Canada before moving to California as a teenager. She has taught history and literature classes to college students, and reading and writing classes to young adults. She is a writer and editor and has been a member of the Start-to-Finish team for several years.

Helen has loved animals and the outdoors since she was a child. She spends many hours chasing after her dog, Ella, on the hiking trails near their home in Los Angeles.

About the Narrator

Barbara Figgins graduated from Northwestern University with a degree in Theatre and has worked at many theaters across the country. She has also worked in film, television and radio. Being a part of this project has been great fun and educational as well! It is always nice to learn something new.

A Note to the Teacher

Start-to-Finish Core Content books are designed to help students achieve success in reading to learn. From the provocative cover question to the carefully structured and considerate text, these books promote inquiry, active engagement, and understanding. Not only do students learn curriculum-relevant content, but they learn how to read with understanding. Here are some of the features that make these books such powerful aids in teaching and learning.

Structure That Supports Inquiry and Understanding

Core Content books are carefully structured to encourage students to ask questions, identify main ideas, and understand how ideas relate to one another. The structural features of the Blue Core Content books include the following:

- **"Introduction"**: A concise introduction engages students in the book's topic and explicitly states the book's themes.
- **Clearly focused chapters:** Each of the following chapters focuses on a single topic at a length that makes for a comfortable session of reading.
- **"Questions This Chapter Will Answer"**: Provocative questions following the chapter title reflect the chapter's main ideas. Each question corresponds to a heading within the chapter.
- **Chapter introduction:** An engaging opening leads to a clear statement of the chapter topic.
- **Carefully worded headings:** The headings within each chapter are carefully worded to signal the main idea of the section and reflect the opening questions.
- **Clear topic statements:** Within each chapter section, the main idea is explicitly stated so that students can distinguish it from supporting details.
- **"Chapter Summary"**: A brief summary recaptures the main ideas signaled by the opening questions, text headings, and topic statements.

Text That Is Written for Success™

Every page of a Core Content book is the product of a skilled team of educators, writers, and editors who understand your students' needs. The text features of these books include the following:

- **Mature treatment of grade level curriculum:** Core Content is age and grade-appropriate for the older student who is actively acquiring reading skills. The books also contain information that may be new to any student in the class, empowering Core Content readers to contribute interesting information to class discussions.
- **Idioms and vocabulary:** The text limits the density of new vocabulary and carefully introduces new words, new meanings of familiar words, and idioms. New subject-specific terms are bold-faced and included in the Glossary.
- **Background knowledge:** The text assumes little prior knowledge and anchors the reader using familiar examples and analogies.
- **Sentence structure:** Blue level text introduces a greater variety of complex sentences than are used at the easier Gold level to help students make a transition to the language of traditional textbooks.

For More Information

To find out more about Start-to-Finish Core Content, visit www.donjohnston.com for full product information, standards and research base.